# Reading for Every Child
# Fluency

## Grade 1

by
Lori De Goede

Published by Instructional Fair
an imprint of
**Frank Schaffer Publications**®

## Instructional Fair

Author: Lori De Goede
Editor: Rebecca Warren
Interior Designer: Lori Kibbey

## Frank Schaffer Publications®

Instructional Fair is an imprint of Frank Schaffer Publications.

Send all inquiries to:
Frank Schaffer Publications
8720 Orion Place
Columbus, Ohio 43240

*Reading for Every Child: Fluency*—grade 1

ISBN: 0-7424-2821-4

4 5 6 7 8 9 10 PAT 10 09 08

# Table of Contents

# Reading First

## Introduction

The Reading First program is part of the No Child Left Behind Act. This program is based on research by the National Reading Panel that identifies five key areas for early reading instruction—phonemic awareness, phonics, fluency, vocabulary, and comprehension.

## Phonemic Awareness

Phonemic awareness focuses on a child's understanding of letter sounds and the ability to manipulate those sounds. Listening is a crucial component, as the emphasis at this level is on sounds that are heard and differentiated in each word the child hears.

## Phonics

After students recognize sounds that make up words, they must then connect those sounds to *written* text. An important part of phonics instruction is systematic encounters with letters and letter combinations.

## Fluency

Fluent readers are able to recognize words quickly. They are able to read aloud with expression and do not stumble over words. The goal of fluency is to read more smoothly and with *comprehension.*

## Vocabulary

In order to understand what they read, students must first have a solid base of vocabulary words. As students increase their vocabulary knowledge, they also increase their comprehension and fluency.

## Comprehension

Comprehension is "putting it all together" to understand what has been read. With both fiction and nonfiction texts, students become active readers as they learn to use specific comprehension strategies before, during, and after reading.

# Getting the Facts on Fluency

## Fluency Basics

Fluency is the ability to read text smoothly and accurately. The reader does not focus on decoding individual words, but on what the text as a whole means. A fluent reader can recognize words, use appropriate phrasing, and read with expression. In order for students to become fluent readers, they need plenty of practice reading aloud. There are other things you can do to help build fluency:

- Read aloud to your students on a regular basis. (You will be modeling fluency for them as you read.)

- Use poetry that has rhythm and rhyming.

- Do choral reading as a whole group and in small groups.

- Perform readers' theaters.

- Use texts appropriate for each student's level.

- Read the text multiple times.

- Pair up with older reading buddies or peers.

Fluency is a difficult skill to teach and assess. This book offers practical first-grade activities to use with your students and straightforward rubrics to guide you in assessing fluency development.

---

### Key Questions for Determining the Level of Fluency

Does the text seem appropriate for the student?

Does the student recognize most words automatically?

Does the student read in phrases?

Does the student recognize punctuation and adjust reading accordingly?

Does the student read with expression?

---

# Stages of Reading

Movement toward the fluent stage of reading will be a gradual process, and each step along the way is important. The majority of your first graders should be in the emergent or early stage of reading, though you may also have students at the pre-emergent and fluent stages.

## Pre-Emergent

A student who is just beginning to learn to read is in the pre-emergent stage. A pre-emergent reader will:

- pretend to read
- know most letter sounds
- participate in reading familiar books
- use illustrations to tell stories
- memorize pattern books and familiar books
- rhyme and play with words

## Emergent

An emergent reader has gained more skills and is demonstrating a beginning reading ability. An emergent reader will:

- identify self as a reader
- retell main idea of simple stories
- read books with word patterns
- rely on print and illustration
- know most letter sounds

## Early

The early reader has made the transition from emergent, but still needs additional skills to become a fluent reader. The early reader will:

- rely on print more than illustrations
- recognize sight words
- use sentence structure clues
- begin to read silently
- read for meaning
- retell the beginning, middle, and end of a story
- use phonetic skills
- understand basic punctuation

## Fluent

A fluent reader at the elementary level has developed many reading skills and can apply them effectively to what is read. Most second graders will not be at this stage. The fluent reader will:

- read beginning chapter books
- retell plot, characters, and events
- use reading strategies appropriately
- read silently for short periods of time
- make connections between reading, writing, and experiences

# Putting It All Together

### Vocabulary

In order to become fluent readers, students need an extensive base of vocabulary words to draw from as they read. You will expose them to a large variety of words over the school year. These words can come from stories they are reading, science lessons, social studies activities, and many other learning experiences. Students need repeated exposure to vocabulary words used *in context*.

### Comprehension

As your students take the final steps toward reading fluency, it is important to make sure they understand what they read. Remember, the goal of fluency is not simply to read faster and faster, but to read *with understanding*. You may find students who become more fluent in their pace and expression as they read, but still struggle to articulate the meaning of what they have read. Follow reading times with questions that focus on the meaning of the text (see pages 56–61).

# Assessing Fluency

One of the best and easiest ways to assess students' reading fluency is to listen to each child in your class read. You can take note of word recognition, speed, expression, and comprehension from just one short reading period spent one-on-one with a student. Another way to assess fluency is to use rubrics. Pages 10–15 contain rubrics for both teacher and student use; each one is described below.

## NAEP Oral Reading Scale

The NAEP scale (see page 10) allows you to track how students relate fluency to comprehension. Are they reading word by word, spending most of their effort on decoding words? Are they reading fluently, attending to the author's meaning as they go? Assigning a level at the beginning of the year and end of the year gives you a way to track student progress.

## Speedy Word Recognition

Create five rows of six irregular words (words that are difficult to decode phonetically). Each row has the same words, but in a different order (see sample below). Briefly review the words prior to beginning the assessment. The students are timed for one minute as they read the rows of words. Count and record the number of correct words. The students can graph their results to monitor progress (see page 11).

**Example:**

| | | | | |
|---|---|---|---|---|
| who | once | of | were | been |
| of | been | again | been | who |
| again | who | been | who | of |
| once | of | were | of | again |
| were | again | who | once | were |
| been | were | once | again | been |

## Progress Profile

Repeated readings of a text are important to develop fluency. For the progress profile rubric (see page 12), the same text is read for one minute each time. Record the date of the reading, the number of words read in one minute, and the number of errors made. The goal is to have the number of words read increase and the number of errors made decrease. Encourage the student to continue working with the text in between timed reading assessments.

## Minute Reading

Using the same text, the student reads for one minute. The partner (peer or older student) helps keep the time with a stopwatch. After one minute has passed, the students count the total number of words read and record it on the chart (see page 13). This gives students a way to track their progress after repeated readings.

## Pair and Share Reading

For this activity, students pair with a partner to read their books. The students take turns reading; each student reads a total of three times. On the rubric (see page 14), students will assess their own reading and also their partner's reading.

## Fluency Self-Assessment

The self-assessment rubric (see page 15) provides a way for students to reflect on their own fluency skills after they read. By drawing attention to things like sounding out words, stopping at punctuation, and understanding what is read, you help students understand the qualities of fluent reading and monitor their own progress toward that goal.

 **Fluency**

# NAEP Oral Reading Fluency Scale

| | |
|---|---|
| **Level 4** | Reads primarily in larger, meaningful phrase groups. Although some regressions, repetitions, and deviations from text may be present, these do not appear to detract from the overall structure of the story. Preservation of the author's syntax is consistent. Some or most of the story is read with expressive interpretation. |
| **Level 3** | Reads primarily in three- or four-word phrase groups. Some smaller groupings may be present. However, the majority of phrasing seems appropriate and preserves the syntax of the author. Little or no expressive interpretation is present. |
| **Level 2** | Reads primarily in two-word phrases with some three- or four-word groupings. Some word-by-word reading may be present. Word groupings may seem awkward and unrelated to larger context of sentence or passage. |
| **Level 1** | Reads primarily word by word. Occasional two-word or three-word phrases may occur, but these are infrequent and/or they do not preserve meaningful syntax. |

Source: U.S. Department of Education, National Center for Education Statistics. *Listening to Children Read Aloud,* 15. Washington, D.C.: 1995.

# Speedy Word Recognition

Student Name _____

**WPM**

30

25

20

15

10

5

**Date**

Words Tested _____

# Progress Profile

Student Name_____ Date _____

Name of Passage _____

## Date

| WPM | | | | | | | | | | | | | | Errors |
|---|---|---|---|---|---|---|---|---|---|---|---|---|---|---|
| 100 | | | | | | | | | | | | | | 20 |
| 95 | | | | | | | | | | | | | | 19 |
| 90 | | | | | | | | | | | | | | 18 |
| 85 | | | | | | | | | | | | | | 17 |
| 80 | | | | | | | | | | | | | | 16 |
| 75 | | | | | | | | | | | | | | 15 |
| 70 | | | | | | | | | | | | | | 14 |
| 65 | | | | | | | | | | | | | | 13 |
| 60 | | | | | | | | | | | | | | 12 |
| 55 | | | | | | | | | | | | | | 11 |
| 50 | | | | | | | | | | | | | | 10 |
| 45 | | | | | | | | | | | | | | 9 |
| 40 | | | | | | | | | | | | | | 8 |
| 35 | | | | | | | | | | | | | | 7 |
| 30 | | | | | | | | | | | | | | 6 |
| 25 | | | | | | | | | | | | | | 5 |
| 20 | | | | | | | | | | | | | | 4 |
| 15 | | | | | | | | | | | | | | 3 |
| 10 | | | | | | | | | | | | | | 2 |
| 5 | | | | | | | | | | | | | | 1 |
| | WPM | E | WPM | E | WPM | E | WPM | E | WPM | E | WPM | E | |

# Minute Reading

Student Name _____ Date _____

Name of Passage _____

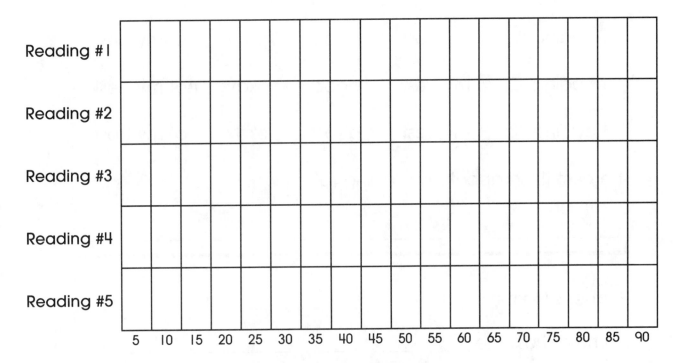

Reading #1

Reading #2

Reading #3

Reading #4

Reading #5

5  10  15  20  25  30  35  40  45  50  55  60  65  70  75  80  85  90

## Words per Minute

**13**

0-7424-2821-4 *Reading for Every Child: Fluency*

# Pair and Share Reading

Student Name _____ Date_____

Name of Passage _____

How well I read (circle one):

Reading #1:     my best     good     okay     not my best

Reading #2:     my best     good     okay     not my best

Reading #3:     my best     good     okay     not my best

The best thing about my reading today was

_____.

Partner's Name _____ Date_____

Name of Passage _____

Reading #1                    Listen to your partner read.

Reading #2    Reading #3    My partner's reading got better because—

_____  _____        it was smoother.

_____  _____        it had more expression.

_____  _____        my partner knew more words.

_____  _____        my partner stopped more for punctuation.   STOP

Student Name _____ Date _____

Name of Passage _____

# Fluency Self-Assessment

Answer the following questions after you read a passage and/or section of a book.

1.  I stopped at all periods.

    yes        sometimes        no

2.  I made my voice louder or softer.

    yes        sometimes        no

3.  I knew most of the words in the passage.

    yes        sometimes        no

4.  I had to sound out words in the passage.

    yes        sometimes        no

5.  I understood what I read.

    yes        sometimes        no

# Using Readers' Theaters

Readers' theaters are a wonderful activity to use for fluency development. To prepare for the performance, students read the text many times. In addition to practice with the written text, students also focus on presentation skills—reading smoothly and with expression, using a clear voice, and following stage directions.

When creating readers' theaters to use in the classroom, it is important to pick stories that will be easy for the students to read (either at their independent or instructional levels). The goal is to have all students feel successful no matter what their reading ability. The more you read the story aloud to the class as a group, the more comfortable they will be saying their lines alone.

Each student eventually takes on the role of a character from the story and speaks their character's lines. (For beginning readers, you can simplify the lines as necessary.) A narrator can fill in the descriptive story action or describe other off-stage events. Long narrations can be divided into two or more narrator roles.

## Creating Readers' Theaters for the Classroom

*Monday*

- Teacher reads aloud three new stories. (Have scripts prepared ahead of time.)
- Assign students to three different groups.
- Pass out scripts to each student in the group.
- No roles are assigned at this time.
- Encourage students to take an extra script home to practice reading their lines aloud.

*Tuesday*

- Students meet in their groups to read through the script several times.
- Highlight one role on one of the scripts, another role on another script, and continue until all scripts in the group have a different role highlighted.
- Read through once. Continue reading, with students switching parts each time until students have read each role at least once.
- Teacher circulates between groups to coach and provide feedback.

*Wednesday*

- Read and have students switch roles (same as Tuesday).
- In the last five to ten minutes, have students choose their roles. If you wish to keep roles assigned by reading level, you can choose roles ahead of time for students.

*Thursday*

- Practice reading multiple times for production on Friday.
- Have students make headbands or neck banners that clearly identify their roles (with name and drawing of the character). This makes it easier for the audience to follow along with the action.
- Do a dress rehearsal. Practice reading lines together and decide where each person needs to stand for each scene.

*Friday*

- Perform!
- Invite other classes, principal, support staff, parents, or neighbors from the community!

## Readers' Theater Character Reading Levels

Each character in the readers' theaters will have a corresponding level. This level can be helpful when assigning parts to students with different reading levels.

Level 1—a support character with few lines at a beginning reading level

Level 2—a support character with average amount of lines at an intermediate reading level

Level 3—a support character with average amount of lines, more advanced reading level

Level 4—a main character with many lines, intermediate to advanced reading level

# Character Worksheet

My name _____

My character _____

My character feels:

happy 😊     scared 😮     mad 😠

excited 😆     silly 😝

My character is:

nice 😊     mean 😠

My character has _____ lines in the readers' theater.
When I read, I think the lines are:

easy to read          okay to read          hard to read

Create a headband or neck banner for your character.
Write the character's name in large letters. Add a drawing
to show what your character looks like.

# Water Droplet's Adventure

| Character | Level |
|---|---|
| WATER DROPLET (W. D.) | 4 |
| PUDDLE | 2 |
| DROPPY | 2 |
| CLOUD (white and dark) | 3 |
| DRIPPY | 1 |
| LAKE | 1 |

**W. D.**     What a nice day! I just love playing with all my friends in this puddle!

**PUDDLE**   You better enjoy it while it lasts, Water Droplet!

**W. D.**     What do you mean, Puddle?

**PUDDLE**   Soon you will take a ride up, up, up into the sky.

**W. D.**     Why do I have to leave?

**PUDDLE**   That's **evaporation** for you! The sun warms us up and we go up to the sky.

**W. D.**     Thanks for letting me know! Oh, here comes the sun! It's getting warm . . . Here I go!

**PUDDLE**   Bye, Water Droplet!

**W. D.**   Wow, that was fun! I wonder what will happen to me now.

**DROPPY**   Hi! What's your name?

**W. D.**   My name is Water Droplet. What's your name?

**DROPPY**   My name is Droppy!

**W. D.**   Nice to meet you! What do you think is going to happen to us?

**DROPPY**   My mom told me we will all come together and form a cloud.

**W. D.**   Oh, I've heard of that! It's a big word called **condensation**. I always wanted to be a puffy cloud in the sky!

**DROPPY**   Me, too! We are getting closer to the other water drops.

**CLOUD**   *(wearing a white cloud)* Hi, kids! Welcome to the group. My name is Cloud!

**W. D. & DROPPY**   Thanks!

**CLOUD**   Soon there will be too many of you and I will become very dark and heavy.

**W. D.**   What happens then?

**CLOUD**   A few of you will need to leave. Then you will be a raindrop. It's called **precipitation**.

**W. D.**      It's getting crowded in here!

**CLOUD**    *(change to a dark cloud)* I'm getting very heavy! I don't think I can hold all of you!

**W. D.**      Time for me to go!

**DRIPPY**   Me, too! My name is Drippy! What's yours?

**W. D.**      I'm Water Droplet! Oh, I think we are landing in a lake!

**DRIPPY**   I'm scared! There are a lot of water drops down there!

**W. D.**      Don't worry! I'll stay with you.

**DRIPPY**   Okay!

**LAKE**     Hi! Welcome to the lake! I'm sure you will like it here. But, you will not be here too long.

**W. D.**      Why do you say that?

**LAKE**     Soon the sun will warm us up and a few of you will go up, up, up to the sky!

**W. D.**      Oh, no! Not again!

**THE END**

# What's Happening to Me?

| Character | Level |
|---|---|
| **NARRATOR** | 4 |
| **ADULT FROG #1** | 1 |
| **ADULT FROG #2** | 1 |
| **EGG #1** | 1 |
| **EGG #2** | 1 |
| **TADPOLE #1** | 2 |
| **TADPOLE #2** | 2 |
| **YOUNG FROG #1** | 3 |
| **YOUNG FROG #2** | 3 |

**NARRATOR**       Two frogs were hopping next to a cool pond.

**ADULT FROG #1**  What a nice day! I love the warm sun!

**ADULT FROG #2**  Me, too. What are you going to do today?

**ADULT FROG #1**  I'm getting ready to lay my eggs in the pond.

**ADULT FROG #2**  Be sure to lay them in a safe place!

**ADULT FROG #1**   I better go now. See you soon!

**NARRATOR**   The adult frog jumps in the pond to find a nice place to lay her eggs.

**EGG #1**   Hey, where am I?

**EGG #2**   I'm not sure. I think we are in the water.

**EGG #1**   There seems to be a big group of us.

**EGG #2**   I think I can get free! Can you?

**EGG #1**   Yes, I can, too! We have tails now. Let's swim!

**NARRATOR**   The eggs have now hatched and the tadpoles are swimming in the pond.

**TADPOLE #1**   I bet you can't catch me!

**TADPOLE #2**   Yes, I can! Here I come!

**TADPOLE #1**   Wee! It sure is fun swimming in the pond!

**TADPOLE #2**   It is a lot of fun, but we have to stay away from the fish. We don't want to be their lunch!

**TADPOLE #1**   No way! Hey, what are those things by your head?

**TADPOLE #2**   They are my new front legs. They will get bigger.

**TADPOLE #1**     I can't wait until we both get our front legs and back legs! Then we can go up land. Let's go swim some more!

**NARRATOR**     The tadpoles' front and back legs grow to be full size, but they still have a small tail. After a little while, their tails go away and they become young frogs.

**YOUNG FROG #1**  Let's go look around on land!

**YOUNG FROG #2**  Sounds like fun! We better be careful. There are lots of things that could hurt us!

**YOUNG FROG #1**  We will be careful! If we get hot, we can just jump back in the pond to cool off.

**YOUNG FROG #2**  Okay! Let's go explore!

**NARRATOR**     The young frogs had fun jumping around in the grass and taking cool dips in the pond. Someday they will become adult frogs and lay eggs of their own.

### THE END

# My Life as a Plant

| Character | Level |
|---|---|
| GARDENER | 4 |
| SEED | 2 |
| SEEDLING | 2 |
| PLANT | 3 |
| ROOTS | 2 |
| LEAF | 2 |
| STEM | 2 |
| FLOWER | 1 |
| SOIL | 1 |
| SUN | 1 |

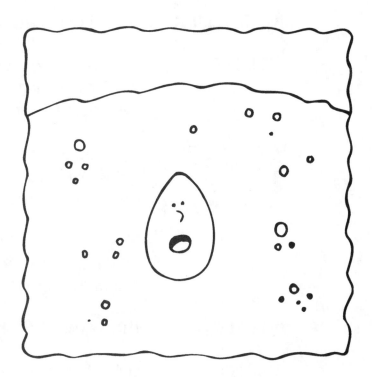

| | |
|---|---|
| **GARDENER** | Spring is here! It's time to plant the seeds in my garden. |
| **SEED** | The gardener puts me in a hole in the soil, covers me up, and waters me. |
| **GARDENER** | I make sure to water my seeds every day. |
| **SEED** | It is very dark under the soil! |
| **GARDENER** | After a little time, the seeds sprout and become seedlings. |

0-7424-2821-4 *Reading for Every Child: Fluency*

| | |
|---|---|
| **SEEDLING** | I am a seedling now. I have a little stem that sticks out of the soil. |
| **GARDENER** | Now I can see where all my seeds are! |
| **SEEDLING** | A little leaf grows from my stem. That will help me make food. |
| **GARDENER** | The seedling keeps growing and becomes a plant. |
| **PLANT** | Now I am a plant. I have a stem that helps me stand tall. |
| **STEM** | That's me! I'm the stem. I hold the plant up. |
| **PLANT** | I also have some leaves. |
| **LEAF** | Hi! I'm a leaf. I help make food for the plant. |
| **PLANT** | Down under the soil, I have roots. |
| **ROOTS** | I'm the roots. I get water from the soil for the plant. I also hold the plant in the ground. |
| **PLANT** | I also have some flowers. |
| **FLOWER** | Look at me! I'm a beautiful flower! I make more seeds so new plants can grow. |
| **PLANT** | All my parts help so I can live and grow. But we can't do it alone. |

**SOIL**   I'm the soil. I give the plant a place to live. I also have water and minerals for the plant.

**ROOTS**   That is where I help! I take the water and minerals from the soil and bring them into the plant.

**STEM**   And I carry the water and minerals to the leaves.

**LEAF**   Then I take the water and minerals, add sunlight, and make food for the plant.

**SUN**   I'm the sun. I keep the plants warm and help the leaves make food.

**PLANT**   It takes work from many things to make me grow. Thanks for all of your help!

**THE END**

# Using Pattern Books

Pattern books are great to use with beginning readers. As the reader moves from page to page, only one or two words change. This is an excellent fluency activity because the repetition means there are limited words to decode. The pictures in pattern books should be very supportive in helping students predict the change in words.

Your students can create their own pattern books. Provide a sentence starter and have each student complete a page. Bind all the pages into a book and put it in a basket in the reading area. These are sure to become favorites with your students!

**Sentence Starter: In the fall, I like to** _____ .

# Just Can't Wait!

"Are we going to the zoo today, Mom?"

"No, Billy. Today is Sunday. We will go on Saturday."

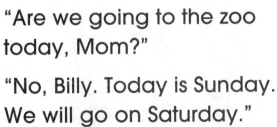

1

**29** 0-7424-2821-4 *Reading for Every Child: Fluency*

"Are we going to the zoo today, Mom?"

"No, Billy. Today is Monday. We will go on Saturday."

2

"Are we going to the zoo today, Mom?"

"No, Billy. Today is Tuesday. We will go on Saturday."

3

"Are we going to the zoo today, Mom?"

"No, Billy. Today is Wednesday. We will go on Saturday."

4

"Are we going to the zoo today, Mom?"

"No, Billy. Today is Thursday. We will go on Saturday."

5

0-7424-2821-4 *Reading for Every Child: Fluency*

"Are we going to the zoo today, Mom?"

"No, Billy. Today is Friday.
We will go on Saturday."

6

"Are we going to the zoo today, Mom?"

"Yes we are! Today is Saturday. Let's go!"

7

# Spider's Busy Week

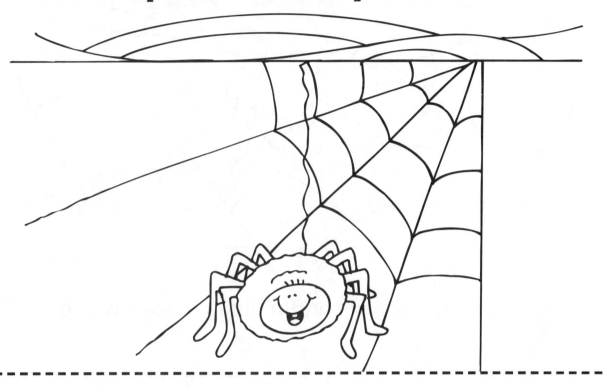

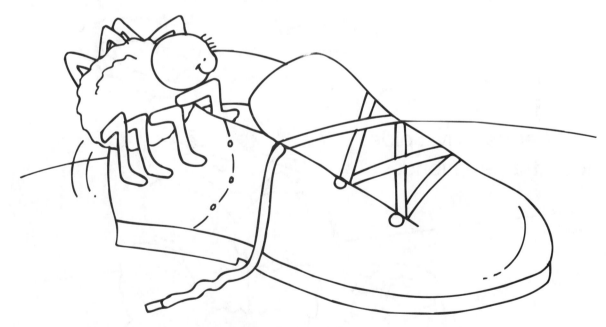

On Monday, Spider found a new home.

1

0-7424-2821-4 *Reading for Every Child: Fluency*

On Tuesday, Spider found a place to take a nap.

2

On Wednesday, Spider found a new friend.

3

On Thursday, Spider found a place to take a bath.

4

On Friday, Spider found a way to have some fun!

5

# Using Silly Rhyming Books

Silly rhyming books are fun to use as you are studying different phonics patterns. The students really enjoy coming up with make-believe words that rhyme with real words. It is also fun for the students to create pictures to go along with the silly words. This is a great fluency activity because students get practice sounding out unknown words and have the support of another rhyming word to help them decode.

To create your own silly rhyming books, list words from the phonics pattern you are working with. Then make up silly words to rhyme with other words. Put the two words—one real and one silly—into sentences and illustrate. First graders love this activity as they play with sounds in words!

# Crazy "Short A" Creatures

The zat put on a hat.

1

0-7424-2821-4 *Reading for Every Child: Fluency*

A fland jumped in the sand.

**2**

The yan sat on the can.

**3**

A tram got stuck in the jam.

4

The blap went to bed for a nap.

5

0-7424-2821-4 *Reading for Every Child: Fluency*

# Crazy "Long I" Creatures

The flike rode a blue bike.

1

A snize got first prize.

2

The drime ate a big, green lime.

3

A blite went to fly a kite.

4

The grile put on a big smile.

5

# Using Build-Up Books

With build-up books, students read words that are repeated from page to page. Some build-up books add new items as you read the story and some start far away and get closer. These help reading fluency because the students have fewer new words to decode on each page.

Students can make their own build-up books for any topic. Provide them the desired framework and have them fill in the missing words and illustrate. You can also use sequencing cards as the sample illustration and have students write a description to show what has changed in each picture.

# Time to Scare the Crows!

Time to scare some crows! First, put on my shirt.

1

After my shirt, put on my pants.

2

After my pants, put on my boots.

3

After my boots, put on my hat.

4

After my hat, put on my scary face! Look out crows!

5

# Looking Closer

In the state, there is a city.

1

Published by Instructional Fair. Copyright protected.    0-7424-2821-4 *Reading for Every Child: Fluency*

In the city, there is a school.

2

In the school, there is a classroom.

3

In the classroom, there is a teacher . . .

4

. . . who teaches me!

5

# Using Rebus Stories

Rebus stories are great to use with beginning readers, who may recognize sight words and some phonics patterns, but not other words that are important to the story. Using a picture above the word allows student to read more fluently through the entire story. The picture also creates a link in students' minds between the vocabulary word and its meaning.

You can easily create rebus stories to use with your students. Find a good clip art book, Web site, or CD to come up with pictures for difficult vocabulary words in the story. If you are feeling creative, you can even draw the pictures yourself!

# Fall Is Fantastic!

In the fall, it is time to go to  school . I put my  pencils ,

 crayons ,  glue , and  scissors in my new  backpack .

I can't wait to meet my  teacher and make new  friends !

I see lots of  trees with red, orange, yellow, and brown

 leaves . When the  leaves fall, I  rake them in a

 pile and  jump in!

 Apples are ripe in the fall. I go on a hayride to pick

 apples and  pumpkins .  Corn is ready in the fall, too!

Fall is fantastic!

# Winter Is Wonderful!

In the winter, there is  snow and  ice  Icicles

hang from the  roof . We need to put on a  hat ,

 scarf ,  mittens ,  coat , and  boots to stay warm.

It is fun to 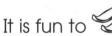 ski and  sled on hills in the winter!

Outside we can make a  snowman and throw  snowballs .

After a day in the  snow , it feels great to drink  hot chocolate

and sit by the  fire .

Winter is wonderful!

# Spring Is Super!

In the spring, the  get new, green  . The
trees                                                leaves

 and  begin to grow, too! You can see
flowers            grass

 eating  .
birds            worms

You can play  ,  , and  in the spring.
tennis            baseball                  soccer

It is fun to ride your  on a  day. When the
bike                    sunny

 blows, it is a good time to fly a  !
wind                                                kite

Spring can come in like a  . There can be
lion                                    storms

with a lot of . Then spring can go out like a with
rain                                          lamb

nice,  days.
sunny

Spring is super!

# Summer Is Spectacular!

In the summer, the [sun] feels hot. [People] like to go to the [beach]. You need to put on your [bathing suit], [sandals], and [sunglasses]. Make sure to bring your [towel] and [sunscreen]! It is fun to build a [sandcastle] with a [pail] and [shovel]. When it is time to go, [ice cream] is a cool treat!

There is a lot to do in the summer. You can ride your [bike], swim in a [pool], go on a [picnic], or play in a [sprinkler]. In July, we put up a [flag] and watch [fireworks].

Summer is spectacular!

# Using Short Reading Passages with Comprehension Questions

Short reading passages with comprehension questions work well with the nonfiction material you teach in other subjects, such as social studies or science. Simplify a nonfiction book or make up a passage of your own. You can include key vocabulary words without having the reading become too lengthy.

It is important to follow the reading passage with comprehension questions to be sure that students understand what they have read. As many readers improve their oral reading, some still struggle with finding meaning in the text. It is important to ask comprehension questions to be sure that students are not just reading smoothly out loud, but also understanding what they have read. No matter how smoothly students read out loud, they are not considered fluent readers until they demonstrate comprehension.

# Magnificent Mammals

When you go to the
zoo, you will see a lot of
mammals. Monkeys,
zebras, lions, and tigers
are all mammals. Bats,
hippos, and goats are
mammals, too!

A mammal has fur
or hair. Mammal
babies are born
alive and drink milk
from their mothers.

**backbone**

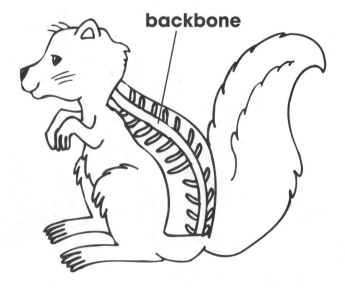

Mammals have a bone
in their back (backbone)
and need to keep their
blood the same
temperature all the time
(warm-blooded).

# Magnificent Mammals, cont.

1.  Name two mammals. _____

    and _____

2.  A mammal has _____ or

    _____ all over its body.

3.  Mammal babies drink _____
    from their mother.

4.  Mammal babies: (circle one)

    a.  hatch from eggs.

    b.  live in water.

    c.  are born alive.

5.  All mammals have a _____ in
    their back.

 **Fluency**

# Beautiful Birds

Look up in the sky! If you are lucky, you may see a bird. Owls, blue jays, and eagles are birds. But not all birds fly. Penguins and ostriches are birds that do not fly.

Birds have wings, feathers, and a bone in their back (backbone). They also have a beak. Baby birds hatch from eggs. Birds need to stay warm (warm-blooded), so many fly to warm places in the winter.

backbone

# Beautiful Birds, cont.

1.  Name two birds. _____

    and _____

2.  A bird has _____ all over
    its body.

3.  Many birds use their _____
    to fly.

4.  Bird babies: (circle one)

    a.  are born alive.

    b.  hatch from eggs.

    c.  live in water.

5.  To stay warm, many birds

    _____ to warm places.

# Fabulous Fish

Oceans, lakes, and rivers are homes for many fish. Sharks, eels, and trout are all fish. Jellyfish and starfish are not fish because they do not have a bone in their back.

Fish have fins and gills. Gills are how fish breathe. They have scales on their bodies. All fish have a bone in their backs (backbone). They stay the same temperature as the water (cold-blooded). Most baby fish hatch from eggs.

**backbone**

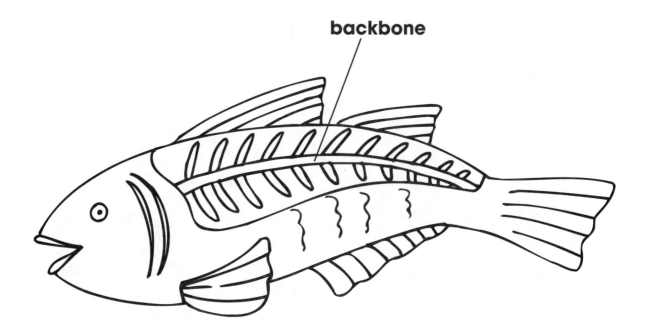

# Fabulous Fish, cont.

1. Fish have _____ all over their
   bodies.

2. A _____ is NOT a real fish.

3. Fish use their _____ to
   breathe.

4. All fish live: (circle one)

   a.  on land.

   b.  in water.

   c.  in a tree.

5. All fish have a bone in their

   _____.

# Using Choral Reading with Two Reading Parts

Choral reading can become mundane after a while. Using choral reading passages with two reading parts spices it up a little! These passages require the students to follow along closely so they can chime in on their part. This also prepares students for readers' theaters.

You can turn any reading into choral reading with two or more parts. It can be as simple as reading every other sentence, every other page, or every other paragraph. How you group students is up to you, but first graders love to be split into boys and girls.

Think about the topics you teach and come up with some choral reading activities of your own!

# Mystery Animals

**Directions:** Choose one student (or one group) to read part **A** and one to read part **B**.

**A**  Knock, knock!

**B**  Who's there?

**A**  An animal with four legs and fur.

**B**  Is it a dog?

**A**  No, this animal lives in the woods and hops.

**B**  Is it a rabbit?

**A**  Yes, it is!

**B**  Knock, knock!

**A**  Who's there?

**B**  An animal with fins that lives in the water.

**A**  Is it a shark?

**B**  No, it is a very big mammal!

**A**  Is it a whale?

**B**  That's right!

# Mystery Animals, cont.

**A**  Knock, knock!

**B**  Who's there?

**A**  An animal with two legs and two wings.

**B**  Is it an owl?

**A**  No, this animal likes to swim. It can't fly, though.

**B**  Is it a penguin?

**A**  You are right!

**B**  One more! Knock, knock!

**A**  Who's there?

**B**  An animal that is big and lives in Africa.

**A**  Is it a giraffe?

**B**  No, it has rough skin and a trunk.

**A**  An elephant!

**B**  Good job!

**A**  That was fun!

**B**  Yes, it was!

# Let's Help the Earth

**Directions:** Choose one student (or one group) to read part **A** and one to read part **B**.

**A**    Time to take out the trash!

**B**    Wow, the bag is very full!


**A**    We sure throw a lot away. What is in here?

**B**    There are some cans, food, paper, and other things.


**A**    Where does all this go?

**B**    The garbage truck takes it to a landfill.


**A**    If we have this much trash, think about how much
         trash goes to the landfill!

**B**    What can we do to help?


**A**    We can start by not using so much of everything.

**B**    Like what?


**A**    Well, we could use regular
         plates and not paper
         plates.

**B**    That sounds like a
         good idea!

# Let's Help the Earth, cont.

**A**   Can you think of other things we can do?

**B**   We can recycle paper, cans, glass, and plastic.

**A**   They can make new things from the used things.

**B**   That will help! Is there anything else we can do?

**A**   We can use things more than once.

**B**   Is that like using jars and tubs to store things, such as buttons or nails?

**A**   Yes, that's a great idea!

**B**   There are lots of little things we can do to help the Earth.

**A**   We can all do our part!

**B**   Let's start now!

# Using Poems

## Poetry for Fluency Practice

Poems can enhance your students' reading expression, fluency, and love for reading! You can never read too many poems! Here are some suggestions for how to use poems in the classroom.

- Provide your students with a poem folder to keep copies of the texts you use in the classroom. A folder with fasteners works the best! The students really enjoy reading these in their spare time and it is a fun keepsake from the school year. It is also a great way to encourage repeated readings.

- Put the poems you use most often on poster board and laminate. It is also helpful to copy them onto an overhead sheet. This makes them easy to read as a whole class.

- Write the lines from classroom poems on sentence strips. You can leave them as whole sentences or cut them into chunks of a couple words each. The students need to put the puzzle back together. These can be stored in a large envelope with a copy of the poem attached to the front for reference.

- Provide your students with a fun family reading experience! Copy poems and send them home with an activity for the family to complete. Another idea is to attach all the poems for the year to heavy paper and laminate. Then rotate the poems so each student takes a different one home each week. This is great reading material to share with parents.

- Highlight a poem that relates to what you are learning as the "poem of the week." It is amazing how many poems you can find that relate to the topics you teach!

- Encourage your students to write their own poetry! Use the poems on pages 69–72 as a guide for some simple poem forms your first graders might try. There is no reason that fluency has to be developed using something someone else has written! Students who wish to share can read their own poems aloud to the class.

# A Week's Worth of Poetry Activities

Use the following structure for the poems on pages 69–72 or any other poetry work you are using in class.

## Monday

Read the poem out loud three times to your students. Ask students several questions about the poem. Have them use highlighters to identify the vocabulary they do not know. Ask students to work in pairs to look up the unknown words. (Some students may actually know all the words in the poem. If they do, ask them to help another student.)

## Tuesday

Read the poem aloud to students. Ask the students several questions about the poem. Have the class read the poem out loud together three times (choral reading). Ask students to illustrate the poem.

## Wednesday

Read the poem together as a class several times. Ask individual volunteers to read the poem out loud. Ask volunteers to act out the poem or certain words in the poem.

## Thursday

Read the poem together as a class several times. Then, alternate reading with the class—you read one line, the class reads the next line (echo reading).

## Friday

Read the poem together as a class. Have students alternate reading the poem in pairs. One person reads, and the other sits with a copy of the poem and marks each time the reader paused (vertical slash line), said a word with emphasis (underline), or stumbled over a word (check mark over word).

# Five Senses Poem

**Directions:** Look at the punctuation in the poem. What do you notice? Read the poem aloud again, using your best expressive voice. Try acting out the poem as you read. Next, create a five senses poem of your own about a different fruit or vegetable. Use the poem below as a model.

### Apples

apples

red, green, yellow

tart and juicky

cold and hard

sweet and fresh

crunchy as can be

apples

0-7424-2821-4 *Reading for Every Child: Fluency*

# Cinquain Poem

**Directions:** Read the poem aloud with your class. As you read along, try to match the speed and expression of the group. What pictures does the poem create in your mind? What messages does the poem give you? Discuss as a class or in groups.

### Spiders

creepy and crawly

spinning, sneaking, and watching

up on my ceiling

spiders

### Rainbows

bright and colorful

shining, glowing, and bending

through the misty sky

rainbows

### Jack-o-Lanterns

orange and round

cutting, scooping, and glowing

shining in my window

jack-o-lanterns

# Pyramid Poem

**Directions:** A pyramid poem describes a person or thing. The first line is the title (one word). Each additional line describes the title and adds one more word. Read the poem below with a partner. Take turns reading every other line (your partner reads the first line, you read the second, and so on).

**Rain**

Rain

Big drops

Fall on me

Get me all wet

Need my umbrella next time!

**& Fluency**

# Two-Word Poem

**Directions:** Listen to your teacher read the poem below. Then read the poem aloud several times. Try to use the same expression as your teacher. Then write your own poem. Use the poem below as a guide.

**Terrific Trees**

round trunk

many leaves

deep roots

long branches

animal homes

tire swings

tree houses

great shade

# Using Punctuation Activities

Punctuation plays an important part in reading fluency. Improving students' understanding of punctuation is key to helping them read more smoothly. Explain to students that punctuation marks are like little signs that tell us to do something as we read. For example, a period is like a stop sign. When we come to the end of a sentence, we stop before going on to the next sentence. As students are learning to read, they need to have practice adjusting their reading for punctuation.

The activities on pages 74–77 are for students to practice reading sentences using punctuation as a guide to expression. You can also easily create similar activities to go along with stories you are reading or topics you are studying in other content areas.

**Fluency**

# Exclamation Points

**Directions:** Add a period (.) or exclamation point (!) to each sentence. Then practice reading the sentences with expression.

1. The dog got his bone

2. Our house is on fire

3. A man is on the bike

4. I like to eat apples

5. Look out

6. The color of grass is green

7. Fish are good pets

8. I love summer

9. Don't touch that fire

10. There are seven days in a week

# Question Marks

**Directions:** Read the sentences and add a period (**.**) or question mark (**?**) to each one. Then practice reading the sentences with expression.

1. What day is it

2. My dog likes to run

3. Why are you so sad

4. Did you see that movie

5. There is a boat on the lake

6. Will you help me

7. You are a good friend

8. She has many friends

9. Can I have that

10. I am in first grade

0-7424-2821-4 *Reading for Every Child: Fluency*

# Periods

**Directions:** Read the paragraphs and add periods at the end of each sentence. Check to make sure that each sentence starts with a capital letter. Rewrite the corrected paragraph on the lines. Then read each paragraph out loud. Pause at the end of each sentence.

## Paragraph 1

it was a hot day my mom said we could go to the beach we put on our bathing suits we packed a lunch, towels, and toys then we got in the car to go to the beach

_____

_____

_____

_____

## Paragraph 2

Bob had a loose tooth he wiggled it and wiggled it he had a hard time eating his lunch it finally fell out before he went to bed

_____

_____

_____

_____

_____

# Quotation Marks

**Directions:** Read each paragraph and add quotation marks (" ") where someone is speaking. Then reread each paragraph, using a different voice for each character.

## Paragraph 1

A butterfly landed on a pink flower next to a buzzing bee.

Hi! said the butterfly.

How are you? asked the bee.

I am hungry, said the butterfly.

Me, too! said the bee.

Let's eat here and then find a new flower, said the butterfly.

Sounds great! said the bee.

## Paragraph 2

Sam got home from school and went to his apartment.

Hi, Sam! said Mom.

Hi, Mom! said Sam.

Did you have a good day at school? asked Mom.

Yes, said Sam.

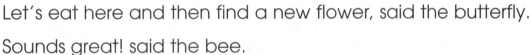

What did you do? asked Mom.

We had a test in math, said Sam.

I bet you are hungry for a snack, said Mom.

Yes, I am! said Sam.

# Resources

## Patterned Literature Books for Reading and Writing

*A Dark, Dark Tale*—by Ruth Brown

*Brown Bear, Brown Bear*—by Bill Martin Jr.

*The Doorbell Rang*—by Pat Hutchins

*Fortunately*—by Remy Charlip

*Goodnight Moon*—by Margaret Wise Brown

*Goodnight, Mr. Beetle*—by Leland Jacobs

*If I Had a Tail*—by Karen Clemens Warrick

*Jesse Bear, What Will You Wear*—by Nancy Carlstrom

*Jump, Frog, Jump*—by Robert Kalan

*One Monday Morning*—by Uri Shulevitz

*Rain Makes Applesauce*—by Julian Scheer

*Squaw to the Moon, Little Goose*—by Edna Preston

*The Very Busy Spider*—by Eric Carle

*Wheels on the Bus*—by Paul O. Zelinsky

*Who Sank the Boat?*—by Pamela Allen

*Why Mosquitoes Buzz in People's Ears*—by Verna Aardema

## Poetry Collections

*A Giraffe and a Half*—by Shel Silverstein

*A Pizza the Size of the Sun*—by Jack Prelutsky

*A Poem a Day*—by Helen H. Moore

*Poems to Count On*—by Sandra Liatsos

*Poems to Grow On: Poetry Activities for Young Children*—by Mabel Chandler Duch

*The Super Book of Phonics Poems*—by Linda B. Ross

# Good Books for First-Grade Reading Teachers

*"Best Practice"? Insights on Literacy Instruction from an Elementary Classroom*—by Margaret Taylor Stewart

*Beyond Storybooks: Young Children and the Shared Book Experience*—by Judith Pollard Slaughter

*Book Talk and Beyond: Children and Teachers Respond to Literature*—editors: Nancy L. Roser, Miriam G. Martinez

*Celebrating Children's Choices: 25 Years of Children's Favorite Books*—by Arden DeVries Post, Marilyn Scott, Michelle Theberge

*Developing Reading-Writing Connections: Strategies from the Reading Teacher*—editors: Timothy V. Rasinski, Nancy D. Padak, Brenda Weible Church, Gay Fawcett, Judith Hendershot, Justina M. Henry, Barbara G. Moss, Jacqueline K. Peck, Elizabeth (Betsy) Pryor, Kathleen A. Roskos

*From Literature to Literacy: Bridging Learning in the Library and the Primary Grade Classroom*—by Joy F. Moss, Marilyn F. Fenster

*In the First Few Years: Reflections of a Beginning Teacher*—by Tina Humphrey

*Journey of Discovery: Building a Classroom Community Through Diagnostic-Reflective Portfolios*—by Ann M. Courtney, Theresa L. Abodeeb

*Reading to, with, and by Children*—by Margaret E. Mooney

*Role of Phonics in Reading Instruction: A Position Statement of the International Reading Association*—by IRA

*Talking Classrooms: Shaping Children's Learning Through Oral Language Instruction*—editor: Patricia G. Smith

*Teaching Phonics Today: A Primer for Educators*—by Dorothy S. Strickland

*Tiger Lilies, Toadstools, and Thunderbolts: Engaging K–8 Students With Poetry,* Iris McClellan Tiedt

*Worm Painting and 44 More Hands-On Language Arts Activities for the Primary Grades*—by E. Jo Ann Belk, Richard A. Thompson

**Magnificent Mammals.....pages 56–57**
1. Answers will vary.
2. fur or hair
3. milk
4. c (are born alive)
5. bone

**Beautiful Birds.................pages 58–59**
1. Answers will vary.
2. feathers
3. wings
4. b (hatch from eggs)
5. fly

**Fabulous Fish ...................pages 60–61**
1. scales
2. jellyfish (or starfish)
3. gills
4. b (in water)
5. backs

**Exclamation Points ................page 74**
1. .
2. !
3. .
4. .
5. !
6. .
7. .
8. !
9. !
10. .

**Question Marks .....................page 75**
1. ?
2. .
3. ?
4. ?
5. .
6. ?
7. .
8. .
9. ?
10. .

**Periods ..............................page 76**
Corrected paragraphs below.

**Paragraph 1**
It was a hot day. My mom said we could go to the beach. We put on our bathing suits. We packed a lunch, towels, and toys. Then we got in the car to go to the beach.

**Paragraph 2**
Bob had a loose tooth. He wiggled it and wiggled it. He had a hard time eating his lunch. It finally fell out before he went to bed.

**Quotation Marks .....................page 77**
Corrected paragraphs below.

**Paragraph 1**
A butterfly landed on a pink flower next a buzzing bee.
"Hi!" said the butterfly.
"How are you?" asked the bee.
"I am hungry," said the butterfly.
"Me, too!" said the bee.
"Let's eat here and then find a new flower," said the butterfly.
"Sounds great!" said the bee.

**Paragraph 2**
Sam got home from school and went in his apartment.
"Hi, Sam!" said Mom.
"Hi, Mom!" said Sam.
"Did you have a good day at school?" asked Mom.
"Yes," said Sam.
"What did you do?" asked Mom.
"We had a test in math," said Sam.
"I bet you are hungry for a snack," said Mom.
"Yes, I am!" said Sam.